RONALD *Reagan*

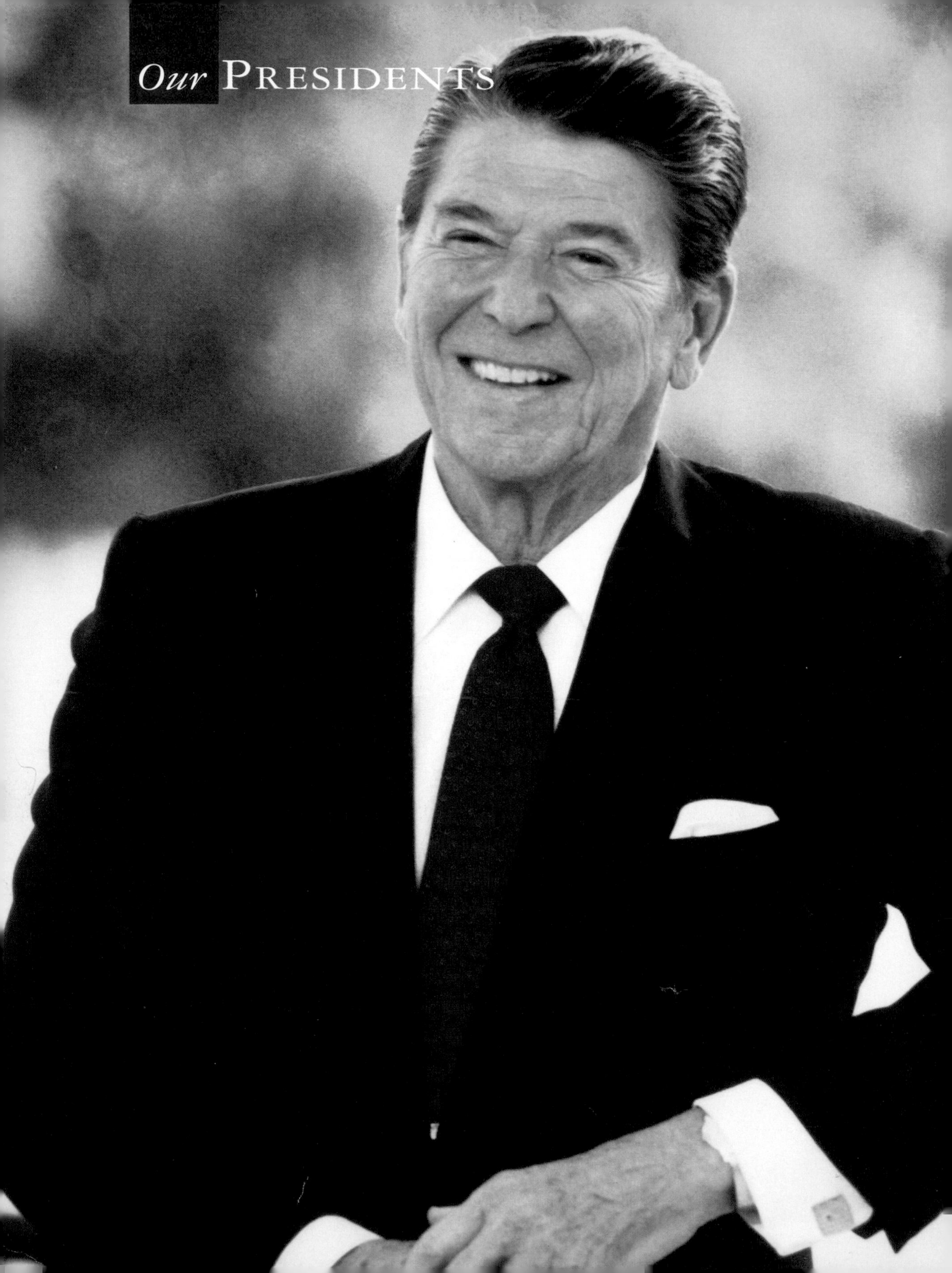
Our PRESIDENTS

RONALD *Reagan*

OUR FORTIETH PRESIDENT

By Cynthia Klingel and Robert B. Noyed

SPIRIT
of America™

The Child's World®, Inc.
Chanhassen, Minnesota

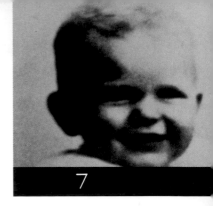

7

RONALD *Reagan*

Published in the United States of America by The Child's World®, Inc.
PO Box 326 • Chanhassen, MN 55317-0326 • 800-599-READ • www.childsworld.com

Acknowledgments
The Creative Spark: Mary Francis-DeMarois, Project Director; Elizabeth Sirimarco Budd, Series Editor; Robert Court, Design and Art Direction; Janine Graham, Page Layout; Jennifer Moyers, Production

The Child's World®, Inc.: Mary Berendes, Publishing Director; Red Line Editorial, Fact Research; Cindy Klingel, Curriculum Advisor; Robert Noyed, Historical Advisor

Photos
All photos courtesy of the Ronald Reagan Presidential Library except page 18, courtesy of the Gerald Ford Presidential Library

Registration
The Child's World®, Inc., Spirit of America™, and their associated logos are the sole property and registered trademarks of The Child's World®, Inc.

Library of Congress Cataloging-in-Publication Data
Klingel, Cynthia Fitterer.
  Ronald Reagan : our fortieth president / by Cynthia Klingel and Robert B. Noyed.
    p. cm.
  Includes bibliographical references and index.
  ISBN 1-56766-874-7 (alk. paper)
  1. Reagan, Ronald—Juvenile literature. 2. Presidents—United States—Biography—Juvenile literature. [1. Reagan, Ronald. 2. Presidents.] I. Noyed, Robert B. II. Title.
  E877 .K58 2000
  973.927'092—dc21
                                                00-011490

14   21   31

Contents

Chapter ONE

The Road to Hollywood

Ronald Reagan's career was unusual compared with other presidents. He went from the movie screen to the Oval Office of the White House. His career was full of interesting events and ended in two terms as the nation's chief executive.

RONALD REAGAN WAS A POPULAR PRESIDENT for many reasons. Some people liked what he did to improve the American economy, which is the financial condition of the country. Others were impressed with how he worked to improve the nation's relationship with the **Soviet Union.** But most Americans will agree that Reagan will be best remembered for his charm, sense of humor, and friendly personality. Reagan often was called "The Great Communicator." He always seemed to have the right words to say, even in sad or frightening situations.

Ronald Wilson Reagan was born in Tampico, Illinois, on February 6, 1911. He was the younger of Jack and Nelle Reagan's two sons. His older brother's name was Neil.

One-year-old Ronald Reagan is shown here with his older brother Neil in a photograph from 1912.

Ronald's family was poor, but his mother always took care of the family's needs. They moved a great deal when Ronald was a young child.

Ronald was a happy boy who enjoyed climbing rocks, hiking through the woods, exploring the countryside, and sledding and ice-skating in winter. Most of all, he loved playing football with his friends. In school, Ronald was a successful student. Not only did learning come easily to him, but the other students liked his friendly, positive personality.

The Reagan family in 1914 or 1915: Ronald (in front of his mother), Neil, and parents Jack and Nelle. Jack Reagan had a difficult time keeping a job as a shoe salesman. His family did not have much money, but Ronald's childhood was still a happy one. In 1920, the Reagans settled in the town of Dixon, Illinois.

Ronald was thrilled that he could be on the football team when he entered North Dixon High School. Unfortunately, he was such a small boy for his age that he sat on the bench most of the season. The following summer, he found a job working for a local construction company. The physical work helped him develop strong muscles. Ronald also started taking swimming lessons and became an excellent swimmer. Over the next few years, as he continued to swim and stay physically active, he grew into a strong, tall young man.

Ronald followed his high school sweetheart, Margaret Cleaver, to Eureka College, in Eureka, Illinois. He was very excited to begin his college career. "I wanted to get in that school so badly, that it hurt when I thought about it," Ronald once said. He took part in many activities at Eureka College. At school, he became interested in acting and found that he loved being on stage. In addition, he worked on the school newspaper and yearbook. Ronald was also a leader, serving as student council president during his senior year.

After graduating in 1932, Ronald decided he would pursue a career in acting. After all, communicating and speaking in front of others came easily to him.

For seven summers, Reagan was a lifeguard at Lowell Park, a local area where people could swim in the river. Several people had drowned before Reagan was hired, and the park had almost been forced to close. Reagan became known as a local hero for saving many struggling swimmers.

▶ When Ronald Reagan was young, he was small compared with other boys his age. When he was in high school, he was 5 feet 3 inches tall and weighed 108 pounds. After high school, he grew to be over 6 feet tall and weighed 185 pounds.

▶ While working as a lifeguard, Reagan saved 77 people.

▶ During his first year at Warner Brothers Studio, Reagan made 10 movies. He played radio announcers in several of these early films. This was an easy role for him to play because of his experience working for radio stations in Iowa and Illinois.

Radio was popular at that time, and he decided to try to get a job as a radio actor. He first looked for work in Chicago. But people told him he needed to get experience in smaller towns before he could get a job in a big city like Chicago. So he drove to Davenport, Iowa, hoping to find work as a sports announcer for WOC radio. The station manager gave him a chance. For 20 minutes, Ronald pretended to announce the play-by-play of a football game. The station manager followed every play as Ronald excitedly followed the action of an imaginary game. The manager was quickly convinced that young Ronald could do excellent work and offered him the job.

Ronald was successful at station WOC. He was soon transferred to a bigger station in Des Moines, Iowa, called station WHO. While there, he had the opportunity to travel with the Chicago Cubs to spring training in California. There he met a Hollywood movie agent. The agent was instantly impressed with Ronald's winning personality and good looks. He arranged for Ronald to try out for a movie role.

Ronald returned to Iowa a few days later and received a message from the agent. Ronald was offered a movie contract with Warner Brothers Studio! It was a seven-year contract, starting at $200 per week. This was a lot of money for a young man at the time. Ronald excitedly accepted the offer, bought a convertible, and headed to Hollywood. He became known as a handsome and popular actor. As always, people liked his warm, happy personality and enjoyed being around him. A hard worker, Ronald was always on time and did a good job.

Ronald Reagan worked as an announcer for WHO radio station in Des Moines, Iowa, from 1934 through 1937.

While eating lunch one day in the studio cafeteria, Ronald met a lovely actress named Jane Wyman. They became friends and soon began dating. In 1940, Ronald and Jane married. Their daughter, Maureen, was born in 1941.

Chapter TWO

A New Career

Ronald Reagan joined the U.S. Army Air Force in 1942. Because of his poor eyesight, he could not become a pilot. Instead, he used his acting skills and made more than 400 training films for the army.

REAGAN'S CAREER AND PERSONAL LIFE WERE going well in 1941. But in December of that year, the United States became involved in World War II. In 1942, Reagan enlisted in the U.S. Army Air Force. His poor eyesight kept him from being a pilot, so he served the army by making flight-training films. When the war ended in 1945, he returned home to Hollywood.

That year, he and Jane adopted a son named Michael. Reagan tried to return to his movie career, but he found it to be much more difficult. Before entering the army, he had been offered roles in large, important films. He was a popular actor. But after returning to Hollywood, he could not find any movie roles.

In 1947, Reagan became president of the Screen Actors Guild. This organization tries to improve working conditions for actors. Reagan worked to get good medical insurance and other benefits for actors. During this time, he had his first opportunity to speak before Congress, asking them to pass laws to help the Screen Actors Guild. This experience sparked Reagan's interest **politics.** While he was becoming more involved in the political world, his wife was enjoying more and more success as an actress. Soon their interests and beliefs were different. In 1949, the couple divorced.

Reagan took several movie parts and continued to stay active with the Screen Actors Guild. In 1951, he acted in *Bedtime for Bonzo,* a movie many people remember for the chimpanzee that was his "co-star."

As an actor, Reagan is best remembered for his 1940 role as football star George Gipp, "The Gipper," in the movie, Knute Rockne–All American. *This was a big Hollywood movie, and audiences loved it. But after leaving the army in 1945, Reagan had trouble finding movie roles.*

▶ Reagan is known for his enjoyment of horses and life on his ranch in Santa Barbara, California. This interest developed after he made a 1946 movie called *Stallion Road*. Afterward, he bought his ranch and made a hobby of working with horses.

Reagan was saddened by his divorce from Jane Wyman. But while working in Hollywood, he met another actress named Nancy Davis. After dating for a few years, the couple married on March 4, 1952.

In 1952, Reagan married an actress named Nancy Davis. The couple had dated for a couple of years and were very much in love. Later that year, their daughter, Patricia, was born. Although his personal life was happy, Reagan's acting career was not as successful.

In the 1950s, television was becoming popular. Reagan thought this might be a new opportunity for him. In 1954, he accepted an offer to host a television program called *General Electric Theater.* This show became an instant success. One of his duties in this job was to visit people who worked for General Electric. Reagan traveled to the company's plants, where the people worked. He talked about being an actor and working in Hollywood. After a while, he started talking about politics, too. He was good at this, and the people liked him. Reagan did this for eight years, until the television show went off the air. Then he was hired to host *Death Valley Days,* which he did until 1965.

By that time, Reagan's life and interests had changed. He was no longer making movies. He and Nancy had a son, Ronald Prescott, in 1958. During his years speaking to the workers of General Electric, Reagan had developed firm beliefs about politics and the future of the United States. He now had strong opinions about how the government should be run. Many people suggested that he run for public office. Although he didn't

Ronald Reagan was the host of General Electric Theater *from 1954 until 1962. The popular television star traveled around the country, meeting General Electric employees. In so doing, he learned that he was an excellent public speaker whom people respected.*

run in an election right away, he did help other **candidates.** Richard Nixon was running for president in the 1960 election. Reagan gave about 200 speeches in support of Nixon, who lost the November election to John F. Kennedy.

In 1964, Senator Barry Goldwater decided to run for president. By then, Reagan had become a leader in California's Republican Party. The Republican Party is one of the nation's two most powerful **political parties.** Reagan was one of two people in charge of Goldwater's **campaign.** To help Goldwater raise money for it, Reagan taped a 30-minute speech. It was called, "A Time for Choosing." The speech was shown on television, and people who saw it were impressed with Reagan. He was an excellent speaker, and his reputation as "The Great Communicator" had already begun. Suddenly, other Republicans knew who Reagan was. Many suggested he run for governor of California in 1966, and Reagan agreed.

Ronald Reagan traveled all over California during his campaign. He also appeared on television. On November 8, 1966, he was elected governor of California. He felt it was important to communicate directly with the people of California, and he often televised messages to the people. The citizens of California liked Reagan and his ideas. In 1970, they reelected him as their governor.

Ronald Reagan, son Ron, Mrs. Nancy Reagan, and daughter Patti posed for this photograph outside their home in Pacific Palisades, California, near Los Angeles. As the Reagans enjoyed a happy family life, Ronald's interest in politics began to blossom.

Many of Reagan's friends and supporters urged him to run for president. In 1976, he decided the time was right. But another Republican named Gerald Ford was also running. Ford was the current president, and he wanted to stay in

office for another four years. He won the Republican Party's **nomination** and became their presidential candidate. But Reagan came in a close second. In the election, Jimmy Carter defeated President Ford. Carter was a member of the Democratic Party, the other major U.S. political party.

Reagan thought his chance to run for president of the United States was gone. He had no idea what his political future would hold over the next 12 years. His successful career as a **politician** had only just begun.

Reagan shakes hands with President Gerald Ford, the Republican Party's presidential candidate in 1976. Reagan lost the nomination to Ford, but he came in a close second. This gave Reagan an excellent chance to win the nomination four years later.

NANCY REAGAN WILL LONG BE REMEMBERED for the support she gave her husband, Ronald Reagan, during his two terms as president of the United States. She took great pride in Reagan's accomplishments and in being his wife. She once said, "My life really began when I married my husband."

Nancy was born in New York City on July 6, 1921. Her name at birth was Anne Frances Robbins. Her family moved to Chicago when she was six. She had a happy childhood in Chicago with her mother, Edith, who was an actress, and her stepfather, Dr. Loyal Davis, who was a surgeon.

Nancy majored in theater at Smith College in Massachusetts. In college, she acted in plays and even had the opportunity to act on Broadway in the play, *Lute Song.* She chose to use the name Nancy Davis as her stage name. Soon she began acting in Hollywood films. Nancy completed 11 films between 1949 and 1956. Her last film, *Hellcats of the Navy,* also starred Ronald Reagan.

After that film, Nancy retired from show business to raise her family. She became involved in many activities when Reagan was governor of California. She was interested in helping people, especially those who were physically and emotionally handicapped. She supported a special program for the elderly called the Foster Grandparent Program and even wrote a book about it.

After her husband was elected president, Nancy used her position as first lady to support the arts and to lead the fight against drug use among young people. She continued this effort long after she and Ronald left the White House in 1989.

Chapter THREE

The Road to the Presidency

Reagan announced his plan to run for president again in the 1980 election. He told Americans that he was running for all people who shared his most important values: "family, work, neighborhood, peace, and freedom."

AFTER REAGAN FAILED TO WIN THE REPUBLICAN nomination for president in 1976, some people thought his goal to become president would never be reached. But Reagan stayed focused on his goal. He set his sights on the Republican nomination for the 1980 election.

Reagan organized a committee in 1978 to help him with his 1980 presidential campaign. Everything seemed to be moving in the right direction. Even though Reagan had a lot of support, other candidates were challenging him—including a former congressman from Texas named George Bush. After early campaign struggles, the Republicans nominated Reagan in the summer of 1980 to be their presidential candidate. Reagan chose Bush to run for vice president.

The opponents of Reagan and Bush were President Jimmy Carter and Vice President Walter Mondale. During their four years in office, Carter and Mondale saw the country go through economic struggles. The cost of products and services across the country had increased greatly, and more than eight million

In the summer of 1980, the Republican Party nominated Ronald Reagan as their presidential candidate. That November, he won the election.

21

people did not have jobs. There were also serious problems with other countries. Iranian **terrorists** were holding 52 American citizens as **hostages,** and Carter had thus far been unable to help them. In the campaign, Reagan criticized Carter for not solving these problems. Although the election was too close to call at one point, Reagan easily defeated Carter to become the nation's 40th president.

Reagan's **inauguration** took place on January 20, 1981. As he was beginning his first term as president, tragedy struck. On March 30, 1981, a man named John Hinckley Jr. attempted to **assassinate** Reagan as he was leaving a hotel in Washington, D.C. The bullets fired from Hinckley's gun wounded a police officer, a Secret Service agent, and Reagan's press secretary, James Brady. When they heard the gun shots, Secret Service agents pushed Reagan into his limousine. The car sped away from the scene. The agents discovered that Reagan also had been wounded. The car rushed him to the hospital. Doctors performed surgery to repair damage to Reagan's chest and one of his lungs. Known for his sense of humor, Reagan said to the

surgeons as he entered the operating room, "I hope you're all Republicans." Reagan recovered quickly and returned to work less than two weeks after he was shot.

One of Reagan's greatest concerns as president was the nation's economy. His plan for improving the economy was to reduce government spending. He believed that the U.S. government wasted a great deal of money. He also wanted to provide large **tax** cuts for individuals and businesses.

During the inaugural parade on January 20, 1981, the Reagans enjoyed greeting the crowd gathered to celebrate the new presidency. In his speech to the nation that day, Reagan urged Americans to "begin an era of national renewal." He said he hoped that the United States would be "a beacon of hope for those who do not have freedom."

President Reagan was up and smiling just four days after the assassination attempt in March of 1981.

News reporters referred to his economic plans as "Reaganomics." Many people criticized his ideas because they reduced or ended programs that helped needy people throughout the nation. Other people believed Reaganomics would lead the nation to a new level of success.

The other area of focus for Reagan during his first term was foreign relations, or the nation's relationships with other countries. His most important goal was to keep **communism** from spreading to new countries. At that time, relations were tense between the United States and the Soviet Union. The Soviets were powerful and hoped to spread their communist system of government to other parts of the world. Reagan spoke against the Soviet Union, calling it an "evil empire." He planned to build the U.S. military and increase the production of **nuclear weapons** as a show of U.S. strength.

There was tension between the United States and other countries as well. In August of 1983, Reagan sent 800 U.S. soldiers to the Middle Eastern country of Lebanon. The soldiers were part of an international peacekeeping effort in the city of Beirut, where people from two religious groups, the Christians and the Muslims, had been at war. Many Muslims did not like having American soldiers in Beirut. On October 23, 1983, a Muslim terrorist drove a truck through the gates of the U.S. Marine camp and crashed into the main building. The truck was filled with bombs and exploded as it hit the building, which was almost completely destroyed. Tragically, 241 U.S. Marines were killed in the explosion.

Two days after the disaster in Beirut, Reagan sent U.S. forces to invade the Caribbean island of Grenada. Cuba, a communist nation and Soviet **ally,** was trying to help establish a communist government there. Fearing for the safety of American students in Grenada and

After a truck bomb killed 241 U.S. Marines, the Reagans honored the victims at a special memorial. Such tragic events made President Reagan even more committed to fighting terrorists around the world.

worrying about the spread of communism, Reagan sent 1,900 U.S. soldiers to attack Grenada. The soldiers battled Cuban and Grenadian soldiers, and the attack was over in a few days. Although many people in Grenada appreciated Reagan's efforts to return peace to their country, his critics wondered whether the attack was necessary. No matter what, Reagan was committed to fighting the spread of communism and to demonstrating the strength of the United States.

On November 2, 1983, President Reagan signed a bill to make the birthday of Martin Luther King Jr. a national holiday. King's family, including his wife Coretta (at left), attended the event. King was a great African American leader who fought for equal rights for all Americans.

As president, Ronald Reagan had several goals to make America stronger. Some of these goals had to do with economics. The number of people working, how much people get paid, and how much people spend are part of economics. How much money citizens pay to the government in taxes and how the government spends this money are also part of economics. Reagan wanted to make changes in these things to strengthen the American economy. His plan was nicknamed "Reaganomics."

Reagan's plan was to have the government spend less money, which would lower the amount of taxes that people paid to the government. In turn, people would have more money to spend. When people spend money, businesses grow, and more jobs are created. This creates a strong economy for a country.

Before Reagan was president, people believed it was necessary to provide programs to help people who didn't have enough money to provide for themselves. These programs cost the government a lot of money. The money the

government spends comes from taxes that the American people pay to the government each year.

Reagan didn't think that these programs were helping people the way they should. He didn't want the government to continue providing such expensive programs if they weren't working well. Without them, the American people would not have to pay so much in taxes.

Reagan believed that if people got to keep more of their money, they could spend it themselves, which would allow businesses in the country to grow. Over time, he believed this would help everyone by creating new jobs. People would no longer need government programs to help them. The president thought this would be more effective than what other presidents had done before him.

President Reagan's changes did have positive results. Many people had more money at the end of his presidency than at the beginning. The way people paid taxes, and how much they paid, also had changed. Many people credit Reagan for a boom in business. His plan for strengthening the country may or may not have been as successful as he had hoped, but he still left his mark on America's economy and will be remembered for Reaganomics.

Chapter FOUR

Ending a Memorable Career

After his first term, Ronald Reagan was a popular president. Most Americans wanted him to hold office for another four years.

AS REAGAN NEARED THE END OF HIS FIRST term in office, he was still popular with many American citizens. Reagan supporters chanted the slogan "Four More Years" as the 1984 presidential election approached.

Reagan and Bush were nominated again as the Republican candidates for president and vice president. The Democratic nominee for president was Walter Mondale, former vice president under Jimmy Carter. Mondale's vice presidential candidate was Geraldine Ferraro, a member of the House of Representatives. She was the first woman ever nominated to run for vice president of the United States. In the 1984 election, Reagan defeated Mondale. He would serve as the nation's president for another four years.

As Reagan began his second term, he faced difficulties with the country of Libya and its leader, Muammar Qadafi. Libya openly supported terrorist groups that targeted Americans. Qadafi continued to challenge the United States. President Reagan continued his firm stance against terrorism. Eventually, he knew he might be forced to use military force against Libya.

But while dealing with Libya and other struggles, Reagan faced a personal crisis. In July of 1985, doctors discovered that he had

President Reagan and Vice President Bush happily accepted the nomination of the Republican Party for the election of 1984.

31

cancer in his large intestine. He had surgery to remove the tumor and part of the intestine. The surgery was a complete success, and Reagan recovered quickly. He returned to work shortly after the surgery.

As 1985 ended, tensions between the United States and Libya continued. Reagan called Libya's support of terrorist groups "armed **aggression** against the United States." In April of 1986, he decided to use military force. U.S. military planes dropped bombs on two Libyan cities in a surprise attack. Other situations involving Libya continued to haunt Reagan as he moved through his second term.

Another significant event during Reagan's second term was the *Challenger* disaster. In the early 1980s, NASA began the space shuttle program, and it was a tremendous success. Twenty-four missions had been successfully completed by the end of 1985. In January of 1986, NASA prepared to send the space shuttle *Challenger* into space. This mission was important for NASA and the country because Christa McAuliffe, a teacher, was part of the crew. This was the first time anyone other than a trained astronaut would go into space.

But shortly after take off, the *Challenger* exploded in the sky. All six members of the crew were killed. The incident shocked the nation. In honoring the *Challenger* crew, Reagan delivered one of his most memorable speeches. His gift for communicating was especially important at that moment. "We will never forget them," said President Reagan, "nor the last time we saw them—this morning, as they prepared for their journey, and waved good-bye, and slipped the surly bonds of Earth to touch the face of God." These words helped people deal with the sadness they felt.

A somber President Reagan addressed the nation from the oval office after the space shuttle Challenger *explosion. His soothing words helped ease the nation's sorrow.*

Relations with the Soviet Union were better during Reagan's second term. In March of 1985, Mikhail Gorbachev became the leader of the Soviet Union. Gorbachev was willing to improve his country's relationship with the United States.

During his second term, Reagan met with Gorbachev several times. In 1987, the two leaders signed a **treaty** that would reduce the number of nuclear missiles kept by each country. This was a big step in helping the two countries create better relations.

One of most difficult times for Reagan was an incident called the Iran-Contra Affair. Some of Reagan's advisors were accused of selling weapons to the country of Iran and then using the money from the sale to help fight the communist government in the country of Nicaragua. The soldiers fighting the Nicaraguan Government were called the Contras. The incident was complicated to understand, and several members of Reagan's staff were forced to quit their jobs because of it. Many people wondered how much President Reagan and Vice President Bush knew about the Iran-Contra Affair. The incident was a difficult situation, but most Americans continued to support the president.

Today, no U.S. president can serve more than two terms, so Reagan did not run for reelection in 1988. Vice President George Bush was elected president. After eight years,

▶ Nancy Reagan sponsored the anti-drug campaign called "Just Say No" to encourage young people to not use drugs and alcohol.

▶ President Reagan enjoyed golf and even practiced his putting aboard Air Force One, the official presidential jet. Another of his favorite activities was watching old movies at the White House.

Reagan left office in January of 1989 at the age of 77. He had often called the United States a "shining city" and did so again in his final speech as president. "My friends," said President Reagan, "We did it. We weren't just marking time. We made a difference. We made the city stronger, we made the city freer, and we left her in good hands. All in all, not bad, not bad at all." Afterward, he and Mrs. Reagan returned to California to live.

In the early 1990s, Reagan was diagnosed with Alzheimer's disease. This disease affects the brain and a person's memory. Since that time, Reagan has made few public appearances. He spends most of his time with his family in California. Mrs. Reagan and Reagan's daughter Maureen have worked hard to convince the government to provide more money for research to find a cure for the disease.

On the last day of President Reagan's term, he and Mrs. Reagan boarded a helicopter at the U.S. Capitol. "I am the same man I was when I came to Washington," he said. "I believe the same things I believed when I came to Washington."

President Reagan took a final glimpse of the U.S. Capitol from the helicopter on January 20, 1989, his last day in office. "It's been the honor of my life to be your president," he said.

Reagan was a president with wit and humor. He is remembered as "The Great Communicator" and for the many memorable and powerful speeches he gave. He is thought of as a president who wanted America to be the strongest and most successful nation in the world. But how would President Reagan like to be remembered? "What I'd really like to do," he once remarked, "is go down in history as the president who made Americans believe in themselves again."

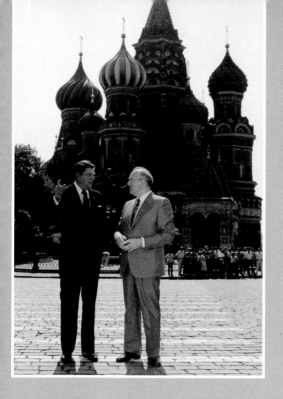

RONALD REAGAN WAS A STRONG BELIEVER IN **democracy,** the kind of government that the founding fathers established for the United States. He believed that it was important for people to have many freedoms. This is one reason he had problems with countries that had communist governments. Communism is a form of government that has great control over its people. Citizens cannot practice religion or speak out against the government, for example. In a communist country, citizens cannot own property. The government owns people's housing and the land where farmers grow crops. The government owns all the businesses in a communist nation. President Reagan believed it was wrong for any government to take away such rights.

During Reagan's first term, he did not trust the Soviet leaders. He was concerned that they were trying to take over other countries and spread communism. But Mikhail Gorbachev became the leader of the Soviet Union in 1985. Gorbachev wanted to change the communist government. He wanted the people to enjoy more freedom, and he hoped to create a better relationship with the United States.

After many meetings, Reagan and Gorbachev signed a treaty to reduce the number of nuclear weapons each country had, making the world a safer place. Reagan also helped convince Gorbachev and other Soviet leaders to end communism in their country. By the early 1990s, the communist government of the Soviet Union was dissolved. Reagan worked hard to have a positive influence on communist countries. By the end of his presidency, he had helped millions of people in the world by working to decrease the threat of nuclear war. His efforts also would help people in communist countries enjoy new freedom.

1911 Ronald Wilson Reagan is born to Jack and Nelle Reagan on February 6 in Tampico, Illinois. He is the youngest of two boys.

1920 The Reagan family moves to Dixon, Illinois.

1928 Reagan graduates from North Dixon High School.

1932 Reagan graduates from Eureka College. He is hired to announce University of Iowa football games for a radio station in Davenport, Iowa.

1934 Reagan becomes the main sports announcer for radio station WHO in Des Moines, Iowa.

1937 Reagan is offered his first acting contract on March 22. After signing, he moves to Los Angeles and begins his movie career. He appears in his first movie, *Love Is on the Air.*

1940 Reagan appears in *Knute Rockne—All American.* He marries actress Jane Wyman.

1941 Japan bombs the U.S. Navy base at Pearl Harbor, Hawaii, on December 7. This action begins U.S. involvement in World War II.

1942 Reagan leaves Los Angeles to join the U.S. Army Air Force.

1945 World War II ends. Reagan returns to Los Angeles and his acting career.

1947 Reagan serves his first term as president of the Screen Actors Guild.

1949 Reagan and Jane Wyman divorce.

1952 Reagan marries actress Nancy Davis on March 4.

1954 Reagan begins hosting the television show, *General Electric Theater.*

1962 Reagan joins the Republican Party.

1964 Reagan makes a televised speech in support of politician Barry Goldwater.

1966 Reagan runs for governor of California. He wins the election and serves until 1974.

1976 Reagan hopes to run for president of the United States, but the Republican Party chooses Gerald Ford as their candidate.

1980 In July, Reagan is chosen to be the Republican presidential candidate. George H. W. Bush is the vice presidential candidate. In November, Reagan and Bush win the election, defeating President Jimmy Carter and Vice President Walter Mondale.

1981 Reagan takes the oath as the 40th U.S. president on January 20. During his inaugural speech, he announces that the American hostages in Iran will be released. He also vows to stop the spread of communism and to improve the nation's economy. On March 30, President Reagan is shot by John Hinckley Jr. outside the Hilton Hotel in Washington, D.C. Reagan is released from the hospital on April 11, 12 days after the shooting. During his first year in office, Reagan begins his plan to strengthen the nation's economy, a plan that later becomes known as "Reaganomics."

1983 On October 23, 241 U.S. Marines are killed in a bombing of their camp building in Beirut, Lebanon. On October 25, Reagan orders U.S. military troops to attack the island of Grenada.

1985 In January, Reagan is inaugurated for a second term as president of the United States. Mikhail Gorbachev becomes leader of the Soviet Union in March. In July, doctors find cancer in Reagan's large intestine.

1986 In January, the space shuttle *Challenger* explodes after liftoff, killing all six astronauts aboard and one teacher, Christa McAuliffe. In April, Reagan orders U.S. military planes to drop bombs on Libya. The Iran-Contra scandal begins when U.S. leaders, including President Reagan, are accused of selling weapons to Iran in exchange for the release of hostages. Money earned from the sale of these weapons was illegally given to anti-communist rebels in Nicaragua to fight their government.

1987 In December, Reagan and Gorbachev sign a treaty in which both nations promise to reduce the number of nuclear weapons they hold.

1988 Vice President George Bush is elected president.

1989 Reagan leaves office at the age of 77.

aggression (uh-GREH-shun)
Aggression is a threatening or violent action against someone or something that has done nothing to deserve it. Libya supported terrorists who committed armed aggression against the United States.

ally (AL-lie)
An ally is a nation that has agreed to help another by fighting together against a common enemy. Cuba was an ally of the communist government in the Soviet Union.

assassinate (uh-SASS-ih-nayt)
Assassinate means to murder someone, especially a well-known person. John Hinckley Jr. attempted to assassinate President Reagan.

campaign (kam-PAYN)
A campaign is the process of running for an election, including activities such as giving speeches or attending rallies. Reagan was in charge of Barry Goldwater's campaign in 1964.

candidates (KAN-dih-detz)
Candidates are people who are running in an election. Before he ran for office, Reagan helped other Republican candidates.

communism (KOM-yeh-niz-em)
Communism is a system of government in which the central government, not the people, holds all the power, and there is no private ownership of property. Reagan wanted to stop the spread of communism.

democracy (deh-MOK-ruh-see)
A democracy is a nation in which the people control the government by electing their own leaders. The United States is a democracy.

hostages (HOS-tij-ez)
Hostages are people held prisoner until some demand is agreed to. Iranian terrorists imprisoned 52 American hostages from 1979 to 1981.

inauguration (ih-nawg-yuh-RAY-shun)
An inauguration is the ceremony that takes place when a new president begins a term. Reagan's first inauguration took place on January 20, 1981.

nomination (nom-ih-NAY-shun)
If someone receives a nomination, he or she is chosen by a political party to run for an office. Reagan first won the Republican presidential nomination in 1980.

nuclear weapons (NOO-klee-ur WEH-punz)
Nuclear weapons use energy to cause powerful, hot explosions that result in terrible destruction. Reagan planned to increase the production of nuclear weapons to make the United States better able to defend itself.

political parties (puh-LIT-uh-kul PAR-teez)
Political parties are groups of people who share similar ideas about how to run a government. The Republican Party is one of the two most powerful political parties in the United States.

politician (pawl-ih-TISH-un)
A politician is a person who holds an office in government. Reagan was a politician.

politics (PAWL-ih-tiks)
Politics refers to the actions and practices of the government. Reagan first became interested in politics while working for the Screen Actors Guild.

Soviet Union (SOH-vee-et YOON-yen)
The Soviet Union was a communist country that stretched from eastern Europe across Asia to the Pacific Ocean. It separated into several smaller countries in 1991.

tax (TAX)
Tax is money paid by citizens to support a government. Reagan wanted to provide tax cuts for people and businesses.

terrorists (TAIR-ur-ists)
Terrorists are people who use violence or fear to make others agree to do something. In 1979, Iranian terrorists took Americans hostage.

treaty (TREE-tee)
A treaty is a formal agreement between nations. In 1987, Reagan and Gorbachev signed a treaty between the United States and the Soviet Union.

41

Our PRESIDENTS

President	Birthplace	Life Span	Presidency	Political Party	First Lady
George Washington	Virginia	1732–1799	1789–1797	None	Martha Dandridge Custis Washington
John Adams	Massachusetts	1735–1826	1797–1801	Federalist	Abigail Smith Adams
Thomas Jefferson	Virginia	1743–1826	1801–1809	Democratic-Republican	widower
James Madison	Virginia	1751–1836	1809–1817	Democratic Republican	Dolley Payne Todd Madison
James Monroe	Virginia	1758–1831	1817–1825	Democratic Republican	Elizabeth Kortright Monroe
John Quincy Adams	Massachusetts	1767–1848	1825–1829	Democratic-Republican	Louisa Johnson Adams
Andrew Jackson	South Carolina	1767–1845	1829–1837	Democrat	widower
Martin Van Buren	New York	1782–1862	1837–1841	Democrat	widower
William H. Harrison	Virginia	1773–1841	1841	Whig	Anna Symmes Harrison
John Tyler	Virginia	1790–1862	1841–1845	Whig	Letitia Christian Tyler / Julia Gardiner Tyler
James K. Polk	North Carolina	1795–1849	1845–1849	Democrat	Sarah Childress Polk

President	Birthplace	Life Span	Presidency	Political Party	First Lady
Zachary Taylor	Virginia	1784–1850	1849–1850	Whig	Margaret Mackall Smith Taylor
Millard Fillmore	New York	1800–1874	1850–1853	Whig	Abigail Powers Fillmore
Franklin Pierce	New Hampshire	1804–1869	1853–1857	Democrat	Jane Means Appleton Pierce
James Buchanan	Pennsylvania	1791–1868	1857–1861	Democrat	never married
Abraham Lincoln	Kentucky	1809–1865	1861–1865	Republican	Mary Todd Lincoln
Andrew Johnson	North Carolina	1808–1875	1865–1869	Democrat	Eliza McCardle Johnson
Ulysses S. Grant	Ohio	1822–1885	1869–1877	Republican	Julia Dent Grant
Rutherford B. Hayes	Ohio	1822–1893	1877–1881	Republican	Lucy Webb Hayes
James A. Garfield	Ohio	1831–1881	1881	Republican	Lucretia Rudolph Garfield
Chester A. Arthur	Vermont	1829–1886	1881–1885	Republican	widower
Grover Cleveland	New Jersey	1837–1908	1885–1889	Democrat	Frances Folsom Cleveland

President	Birthplace	Life Span	Presidency	Political Party	First Lady
Benjamin Harrison	Ohio	1833–1901	1889–1893	Republican	Caroline Scott Harrison
Grover Cleveland	New Jersey	1837–1908	1893–1897	Democrat	Frances Folsom Cleveland
William McKinley	Ohio	1843–1901	1897–1901	Republican	Ida Saxton McKinley
Theodore Roosevelt	New York	1858–1919	1901–1909	Republican	Edith Kermit Carow Roosevelt
William H. Taft	Ohio	1857–1930	1909–1913	Republican	Helen Herron Taft
Woodrow Wilson	Virginia	1856–1924	1913–1921	Democrat	Ellen L. Axson Wilson Edith Bolling Galt Wilson
Warren G. Harding	Ohio	1865–1923	1921–1923	Republican	Florence Kling De Wolfe Harding
Calvin Coolidge	Vermont	1872–1933	1923–1929	Republican	Grace Goodhue Coolidge
Herbert C. Hoover	Iowa	1874–1964	1929–1933	Republican	Lou Henry Hoover
Franklin D. Roosevelt	New York	1882–1945	1933–1945	Democrat	Anna Eleanor Roosevelt Roosevelt
Harry S. Truman	Missouri	1884–1972	1945–1953	Democrat	Elizabeth Wallace Truman

Our PRESIDENTS

President	Birthplace	Life Span	Presidency	Political Party	First Lady
Dwight D. Eisenhower	Texas	1890–1969	1953–1961	Republican	Mary "Mamie" Doud Eisenhower
John F. Kennedy	Massachusetts	1917–1963	1961–1963	Democrat	Jacqueline Bouvier Kennedy
Lyndon B. Johnson	Texas	1908–1973	1963–1969	Democrat	Claudia Alta Taylor Johnson
Richard M. Nixon	California	1913–1994	1969–1974	Republican	Thelma Catherine Ryan Nixon
Gerald Ford	Nebraska	1913–	1974–1977	Republican	Elizabeth "Betty" Bloomer Warren Ford
James Carter	Georgia	1924–	1977–1981	Democrat	Rosalynn Smith Carter
Ronald Reagan	Illinois	1911–	1981–1989	Republican	Nancy Davis Reagan
George Bush	Massachusetts	1924–	1989–1993	Republican	Barbara Pierce Bush
William Clinton	Arkansas	1946–	1993–2001	Democrat	Hillary Rodham Clinton
George W. Bush	Connecticut	1946–	2001–	Republican	Laura Welch Bush

Presidential FACTS

Qualifications

To run for president, a candidate must
- be at least 35 years old
- be a citizen who was born in the United States
- have lived in the United States for 14 years

Term of Office

A president's term of office is four years. No president can stay in office for more than two terms.

Election Date

The presidential election takes place every four years on the first Tuesday of November.

Inauguration Date

Presidents are inaugurated on January 20.

Oath of Office

I do solemnly swear I will faithfully execute the office of the President of the United States and will to the best of my ability preserve, protect, and defend the Constitution of the United States.

Write a Letter to the President

One of the best things about being a U.S. citizen is that Americans get to participate in their government. They can speak out if they feel government leaders aren't doing their jobs. They can also praise leaders who are going the extra mile. Do you have something you'd like the president to do? Should the president worry more about the environment and encourage people to recycle? Should the government spend more money on our schools? You can write a letter to the president to say how you feel!

1600 Pennsylvania Avenue
Washington, D.C. 20500

You can even send an e-mail to: president@whitehouse.gov

For Further INFORMATION

Internet Sites

Visit the Ronald Reagan Presidential Library:
http://www.reagan.utexas.edu

Visit these sites about Ronald Reagan:
http://www.reaganranch.org
http://www.80s.com/Icons/Bios/ronald_reagan.html
http://reagan.webteamone.com
http://www.its.ilstu.edu/reagan
http://www.reaganfoundation.org
http://www.ipl.org/ref/POTUS/rwreagan

Find more information on Nancy Reagan:
http://www.whitehouse.gov

Find more information on Alzheimer's disease:
http://www.alzheimers.com

Learn more about all the presidents and visit the White House:
http://www.whitehouse.gov/WH/glimpse/presidents/html/presidents.html
http://www.thepresidency.org/presinfo.htm
http://www.americanpresidents.org/

Books

Dunham, Montrew. *Ronald Reagan: Young Leader* (Childhood of Famous Americans). New York: Aladdin, 1999.

Feinstein, Stephen. *The 1980s: From Ronald Reagan to MTV* (Decades of the Twentieth Century). Springfield, NJ: Enslow Publishers, 2000.

Francis, Sandra. *George Bush: Our Forty-First President.* Chanhassen, MN: The Child's World, 2002.

Kent, Zachary. *Encyclopedia of Presidents: Ronald Reagan.* Chicago: Childrens Press, 1989.

Lawson, Don. *The Picture Life of Ronald Reagan.* New York: Franklin Watts, 1981.

Warren, James A. *Cold War: The American Crusade against the Soviet Union and World Communism, 1945–1990.* New York: Lothrop, Lee & Shepard, 1996.

Index